MOURNING: THE JOURNEY FROM GRIEF TO HEALING

MOURNING

The Journey from Grief to Healing

PATRICK M. DEL ZOPPO

ALBA·HOUSE   house   NEW·YORK

SOCIETY OF ST. PAUL, 2187 VICTORY BLVD., STATEN ISLAND, NEW YORK 10314

Library of Congress Cataloging-in-Publication Data

Del Zoppo, Patrick M.
    Mourning: the journey from grief to healing / Patrick M.
Del Zoppo.
            p.   cm.
    ISBN 0-8189-0737-1
    1. Grief — Religious aspects — Christianity.   2. Bereavement —
Religious aspects — Christianity.   3. Consolation.   4. Spiritual
healing.   I. Title.
BV4905.2.D45   1995
248.8'6 — dc20   95-15288
                                                    CIP

Produced and designed in the United States of America by the
Fathers and Brothers of the Society of St. Paul,
2187 Victory Boulevard, Staten Island, New York 10314,
as part of their communications apostolate.

ISBN: 0-8189-0737-1

Printing Information:

Current Printing - first digit   2   3   4   5   6   7   8   9   10

Year of Current Printing - first year shown
            1996   1997   1998   1999   2000

In Dedication

To the people of
the Archdiocese of New York,
who share their dyings, deaths and risings
through an adventure in faith.

Table of Contents

Blessed Are the Sorrowful ix

Prologue xi

Introduction xv
    The Theme of Loss xv
    Understanding the Journey xviii
    The Effects of Death xx
    Mourning Begins the Process xxii
    Mourning Is an Outward Expression xxiii

The First Phase of Grief 1
    Numbness and Disbelief 2

The Second Phase of Grief 5

The Third Phase of Grief 9
    A Time of Confrontation 9
    Psalm 102 11
    Physical Distress 12
    Crying and the Effects of Its Release 15

The Fourth Phase of Grief 17
    Searching, Denial and Distortion 17
    Disorganization 18
    Preoccupation with the Events of Loss 19
    Normal Thought Patterns In Grief 20

The Fifth Phase of Grief 21
    Anger 21
    Guilt 24
    Loneliness 26

Loneliness 27
Helplessness 28
A Review of the Realities of Grief 30

The Sixth Phase of Grief 31
Understanding Your Loss 31
Experiencing the Pain of Your Grief 32
Adjusting to a Changed World 33
Sea Sculpture 34

A Final Word
Loss as an Agent for Change 35
Ideas for the Journey 36
Bereaved Person's Prayer 37
An Affirmation for Those Who Have Lost 38
Psalm 5 39
Psalm 23 40
Psalm 65 40
Psalm 121 41

Bereavement Resources 43

Notes 45

Blessed Are the Sorrowful

In the Process of Grief... They Shall Be Healed

And what does it mean to mourn? I asked the multitude, and an elder stepped forward. To mourn, she said, is to be given a second heart. It is to care so deeply that you show your ache in person. To mourn is to not be ashamed of the tears. It is to be broken, to be built up and to be healed all in the same moment. Blessed are you if you can mourn with an understanding of your own broken being. Blessed are you if you have a heart that feels, a heart that hurts and a heart that loves. And blessed are you if you can understand others with a heart that serves — and a heart that sees the need before it's spoken. To mourn is to forget yourself for a moment and to get lost in someone else's pain — and then to find yourself in the very act of getting lost. To mourn is to be an expert in the miracle of being careful with your pain. It is to be full of willingness and forever reaching out to and picking up and holding carefully others who hurt. To mourn is to sing with the dying and to be healed by the song and by the death. To mourn is to move forward and to look back. To mourn is to say YES!

Prologue

Deep within us all there is an amazing inner sanctuary
of the soul, a holy place, a Divine Center, a speaking
Voice, to which we may continuously return. . . It is a
Light within that illuminates the face of God. . . For the
spiritual person is forever bringing all affairs down into
the Light, holding them there in the Presence, re-seeing
them and the whole of the world. . . in a new and
overturning way.   C.S. Lewis, 1947

Emotional pain is part of life. Healing that pain, especially the
pain after death is both a scientific undertaking in the psychological realm, as well as a sacred religious task. Recently, we have
found complementary and overlapping tasks in both worlds of
healing and caregiving, moving away from the fear that one
might outweigh the other.

Emotional pain after loss affects the total being. It must be
dealt with and touched by something deeper than mere biology,
or neural processes. Most of us in helping professions who sit
face to face with a person in the midst of crisis, are only too aware
that there is something that must be grasped within that individual before a change can take place. This something is just as
indispensable for the behaviorist who speaks in stimulus-re-
sponse terms as it is for the existentialist or humanist who speaks
in terms of meaning. Mere counseling techniques, proven and
wholesome as they are, will fail if something else does not occur
in the counselor's time with the client. Another ingredient must
be added to the process.

There are many prominent writers and researchers, both psychologists and theologians who are eager to talk about this special ingredient which seems so necessary in various aspects of counseling, specifically loss and separation counseling. Some call it a placebo and others a positive expectation. Still, there are others who come from the ranks of psychology and theology who will call this ingredient "spirit."

Hope, positive experience, placebo, relationship and spirit are all attempting to define that seemingly indefinable ingredient called "relationship with God" that takes place along the road to personal recovery. When the sufferer is grasping for more than understanding and storytelling for relief, for more than another's interpretation of the stages of grief — we can be sure that it is the wounded spirit calling out to a familiar entity, God. When confronted with emotional suffering due to loss, the thirst is often for something deeper than our mindful understanding of the bereavement process. Anyone who observes a mourner sees an individual struggling to make sense out of his or her experience. Sufferers seek a way to transcend their chaotic existence. Seeing it from a new angle is not always possible when the healing journey is undertaken in isolation. However, most people will recall that their relationship with their loved one existed out of love and that the love was not created in isolation, but in union with another and within the presence of God. As we grope for a more advantageous realm in which we can view our losses, we see grief as a predicament that can ultimately be transcended through a relationship with God and through relationships with others. In ministry to Christians, a counselor may view the client in discontent because the therapeutic partnership may not be touching the healing potential of hope through a relationship with God. Some grievers have reported feeling boxed in during the therapeutic association in bereavement counseling because of the lack of openness to a hope in God as a life-sustaining and life-giving part of their recovery. Those in grief often struggle for a liberating perspective that will enable them to transcend the reality of their experience and to see the broader picture of their emerging and developing self following the death of a loved one.

A commitment to the spiritual does not deny a commitment to the scientific. One does not replace the other. Rather, the spiritual may be seen to complement and extend the scientific. Pastoral bereavement counseling is a multi-faceted approach to caregiving.

Mourning: The Journey from Grief to Healing invites the reader to befriend the mourning process. The treatment of grief, mourning, and bereavement is meant to be an adventure in faith as well as a personalized education regarding the physical and emotional aspects of recovery after death. The ideas, suggestions and hopes come from a pastoral counselor who believes in a holistic road to healing — a process called mourning.

Patrick Del Zoppo
All Saints Day, 1995

Introduction
Loss and Its Effect on Good People Like Us

Past losses and separations have
an impact on current attachments,
losses, and separations. And all
these factors bear on the fear of
future loss and separation, and
our capacity to make future
attachments.

The Theme of Loss

From infancy our lives have been bound to people, places and
things. In fact, much of current-day personality testing seeks to
know just how well we have been able to integrate our life into
the lives of others in various forms of *attachment*. Having passed
through various developmental stages of life, we may even be
able to recall the patterns our own adjustment took as we
attached ourselves to significant persons, places, objects and
even dreams. Sometimes we were attached to others out of our
need for survival. And as we moved away from infancy into
childhood and adolescence, we may be able to recall how our
attachments were made through personal choice. Developmental psychologist, John Bowlby, gives us a theory regarding the
pattern of human development which portrays the essential
ingredients leading to maturity as stemming from how well we
were able to initiate and maintain our early years of attachment.
Bowlby notes that the basic human needs for safety, security,

trust and personal response are absolutely necessary for matu
rity from early infancy through childhood and adulthood. The
interesting fact is that we continue to seek safety and security
through the relationships that we develop and maintain throughout our lifetime.

As we view our attachments throughout our life span, we
also come face to face with another life reality — *loss*. And from
the same developmental point of view, it is safe, if not obvious,
to say that loss is just as necessary to the human life-cycle as is
attachment. In fact, loss and separation are often the vehicles
God uses to introduce us to a new and more abundant life. But
we human beings don't like separation. It changes us. The
harmony that once nurtured us is now disturbed. The discord
introduced into our existence interrupts the melody which once
enabled us to make sense out of our lives when the attachment
to another human being, a place, an object, a desire or dream,
existed. We protest that discord. It neither sounds right nor feels
right. It makes us uneasy and causes us pain.

Loss is defined as the deprivation of something that we
have had and valued, and includes the experience of being
separated from something important in our lives. It can be
temporary or final. Some losses are obvious, while others are
more subtle. Losses can even paralyze us with fear at times.
However we view loss, or whatever meaning we may later
assign to it, it is safe to say that it is absolutely real and pro-
foundly affects body and mind and spirit at least for a while. Our
perceptions of loss change with time and are affected by our
personality traits, our cultural heritage, our religious and spiritual beliefs, as well as by our education and our social environ-
ment.

Our response to loss is the experience of *grief*. Grief is the
protest of the body, mind and spirit to the severing of an
attachment that has had value for us. The severity of the protest
will be determined by the value that we have placed upon our
attachment. The infant protests the absence of mommy. Mothers
often have a post-partum experience of loss and grieve after

giving birth. Children cry on the first day of kindergarten, and parents have been known to have anxiety attacks when their children move on to college. Wedding days and anticipated births bring tears of joy mingled with a certain grief, and so the human life-cycle is challenged and beset by the reality and need for attachment and loss.

There is one loss, however, that while expected will meet the most severe of all life protests — the death of one whom we have loved. It is in the irreversibility of that final loss that the protest of grief causes the greatest separation pain. On one level our mind is always prepared for the fact that relationships will one day have to come to an end. Our mind flies past that thought, for who among us would want to dwell on such a potentially sad idea and fact of life? And yet, a God who created life through a myriad of attachments and sustains it through a variety of losses comes to our aid again, not to spare us from the effects of grief and the pain of separation that are absolutely necessary, but to bring us to another spiritual level through a process which we call *mourning*. Mourning is the prerequisite for healing. In fact, mourning itself is actually the beginning of a critical journey where grief is acknowledged, felt, understood and expressed. To mourn is to feel the loss at every level of our existence. Is it frightening? The answer is obviously yes. But to mourn means that we are fully alive. You are alive because you have been bound by your attachment to a unique individual who was truly known to you alone. And one of the effects of that attachment was that his or her essence was incorporated into your very being. Hermann Broch in his novel *The Spell* says, "No one's death comes to pass without making some impression, and those close to the deceased inherit part of the liberated soul and become richer in their humaneness." It is that essence that cannot die with death. And while it is absolutely true that an indispensable relationship can never truly be severed through death, mourning will take us one step at a time into a personal conviction of that fact.

We invite those of you who are in mourning to join us in this

step by step journey through the process called mourning which
will culminate in a healing, a healing for your body that hurts, for
your mind and emotions facing the challenge of painful feelings,
and for your spirit that may be crushed by the isolation that you
feel. In the midst of the journey is a promise called hope. Hope
is a wish or desire accompanied by confident expectation of its
fulfillment, a conviction, therefore, that the powers which will
lift you up are much stronger than anything that could hold you
down. You are embarking on a journey from grief to healing
which is understood in the context of hope.

Understanding the Journey

Sometimes death touches us for the first time as a child. Sometimes it is in our teen and young adult years, and for others, the
death of a significant person is met during adulthood. Even
though death is a normal and natural part of the life-cycle of
attachment and loss, it is still spoken of in hushed tones; in
hospital hallways, outside the funeral home, generally in secrecy
and sometimes in knowing silence. While there are many courses
at medical schools in the art of saving lives, there are few courses
on how to tell someone that their loved one has died. How many
of us walk up the steps of a funeral home and still wonder what
words we should use to console someone after their loss. We may
come to the conclusion that this normal part of the life experience
is not so easily accepted as some would think.

Anthropologist Margaret Mead once said that when a
person is born, we rejoice, when they are married, we celebrate,
but when they die, we try to pretend that nothing has happened.
Death is a fact of life. It has always been so. Even Neanderthal
man took pains to mark the death of those to whom he had been
attached in life. He bound them in a fetal position and buried
them with the artifacts they had used during life. This person of
limited vocabulary was saying that this was the end to an
attachment that once existed but which somehow continued

beyond the grave. We are not given entry to his or her feelings, but we can't help wonder what his or her emotions might have been some 60,000 years ago. It is only in this final quarter of the Twentieth Century that we have opened a window of light on the discussion of death and dying.

Though Sigmund Freud spoke in *Mourning and Melancholia* (1917) of helping a patient who lost her father, little else was written until 1943 when Dr. Eric Lindermann related his experiences of working with families after their loved ones died in the tragic fire at the Coconut Grove Nightclub which killed more than 500 young people in Boston, Massachusetts. It was here that we first noticed that caregivers began believing mourners who complained of physical and emotional pain after the death of a loved one. The real ground-breaking work which opened us up to the full reality of grief and mourning, however, was written by Dr. Elisabeth Kübler-Ross in 1968: *On Death and Dying*. A Swiss psychiatrist working in Chicago, she documented the strong feelings of pre-death grief in her terminally ill patients. It was clinically labeled as anticipatory grief.

The finest contribution that the work of Dr. Kübler-Ross made, though, was in the area of methodology in the counseling of dying patients and their loved ones. It was based on the clinical evidence that patients who are dying usually go through a series of stages (denial, anger, bargaining, depression, and acceptance). Some may show signs of more than one stage at any time and may move back and forth between stages. Confronted with the news that they are terminally ill, most patients seek to deny its truth. When they do face the grim reality, they often feel great anger and rage. Many then begin a kind of bargaining process, promising reforms in return for recovery. Depression commonly sets in soon after this bargaining fails to work. If patients receive adequate counseling and support from loved ones, they ultimately accept their approaching death and are able to die peacefully. Dying individuals and their loved ones go through the human grieving process. Although the experience of grieving varies in some respects among societies and individuals, its basic aspects seem to be universal and biological. Counseling today, based on the findings of Dr. Kübler-Ross, is concerned with helping patients and loved ones to grieve naturally without repressing their emotions.

In accepting grief as a reality and fact of life, we are able to try and make sense out of the suffering encountered by all bereaved persons. We are ready to embark on a valid and important journey in faith with many twists and turns as we make our way through uncharted waters toward a place of discovery hitherto unknown. In the process we will learn and grow as we acquire new information about the grieving process and discard old ideas which no longer seem valid at this time. And when the journey gets too rough, we will allow ourselves to be lifted up in spirit by a God who understands because he has made the human journey before us in a different pair of shoes. We will find that, because we share a problem that is not unique to us, others who have suffered the loss of a loved one can often offer us invaluable assistance. In alleviating the suffering of grieving persons, human support, including warmth, open acceptance, empathy and love, is almost indispensable.

The Effects of Death

The death of a significant person in our life creates a time of normal crisis. Loss due to death brings us into a time of transition. Our response is one of *grief*. Grief is a normal and natural reaction to the death of a loved one. Grief will not be a way of life, nor is it a permanent response, although its effects can be long-lasting in duration and intensity. It is not a disease to be cured, but rather a complex set of reactions that are bound to occur following the emotional upheaval caused by death. It is not unlike the trauma that the body feels when physically injured. The wound in grief results from the physical and psychological severing of a relationship that once existed. Of course, memory will later serve in the process of healing and the restoration of joy.

But those who grieve do not feel the comforting effects for quite some time after the loss. It is important to note that we do not choose whether or not to grieve. Grief is an active and normal response and results in one or many reactions. In a later chapter, we will discuss the causes and determinants of our grief responses, but for now let us move one step at a time, slowly and deliberately, through the mourning process.

Individuals grieve, couples grieve, families grieve, and even communities grieve. Recently, a tragic fire in New York City killed three fire-fighters all within the same local area. Of course, we can imagine the effects of such a loss on the family and friends of these brave men, and also on the fire company of the men who served with them. As I passed the firehouse on the way to my office, I was amazed at the huge number of floral tributes and notes left at the large firehouse doors. I was compelled to stop and take a closer look, noting that all of these floral tributes contained notes and messages. One such message said, "You didn't know me, but you spent your life protecting my family by the work you did. Thank you for your act of bravery. My prayers for your family. — Ted, Linda, James and Terry." Loss, all loss, causes us to stop and take notice. Grief is our response to loss. While this family expressed their sentiments to a friend unknown to them, they were expressing a part of a relationship that was severed. A relationship of trust with one who pledged by his life to protect them and their community. Their floral tribute and note was a way of commemorating the relationship that meant something to them. It was also a great lesson for their children.

Grief causes us to stop and to take notice of our feelings, our beliefs, our hopes and our fears. Well-intentioned friends and supporters have been known to try to protect us from our grief by encouraging us to have a "stiff upper lip" or to "be strong." These well-wishers mean no harm, but out of their own feelings of confusion and sense of inadequacy, the words they offer are often the first ones that come to mind. When I question my clients in bereavement counseling and therapy as to what they would like to hear, a common response is, "I wish they would simply sit

with me in silence, or just say, 'How are you today?'" If a friend
were to ask that question, and if you were to be honest about your
thoughts, the questioner may have to listen to some difficult
feelings and that might emerge out of your honesty. The effects
of grief are so taxing that it requires great patience for yourself
and with others. Can you be patient with yourself?

Mourning Begins the Process

While the words mourning and grief are used interchangeably,
they contain different nuances and refer to somewhat different
experiences. As mentioned, grief is the actual physical, emotional, and spiritual response to loss. Mourning is the process of
understanding and expressing the pain associated with the grief
response. Mourning is the living out of the expressions of grief.
It is grief going public. The adjustment process begins with the
acknowledgment that death has actually occurred. Mourning
needs time. Time is a very important aspect of the grief process.
Grief is real and, just as a physical illness needs to run its course,
grief must run its own unique course through the mourning
process. It is a mistake, however, to think that time alone will heal
the wounds of grief. Rather it is how time is used that will play
an all important role in the recovery process. Recovery results
when the mourning process is successful. The catharsis (the
cleansing of the emotions with an accompanying release of
tension and anxiety) is brought about by working through the
painful symptoms, side effects, strong feelings and realities
associated with loss.

Grief is an active, not a passive, part of the mourning
process. It is frightening to many because of the intensity of the
painful emotions which are aroused. Part of the pain associated
with the mourning process is felt when the mourner questions
the normalcy and legitimacy of the pain. We are not accustomed
to the number of emotions that will arise simultaneously or the
intensity and frequency with which the eruptions of grief will

take place. It is hard to imagine, but healing actually comes from our immersion into pain. When a physical wound is lanced by the doctor's instrument, the pain begins to go away. In a similar way, mourning "lances" the wound of grief so that the inner pain may be released. That release is expressed in physical demonstrations of anger, rage, guilt, helplessness, fear and confusion. These strong and repeated feelings must be labeled, felt and expressed during the healing process.

It is important to remember that while we experience attachments and losses throughout our life, we usually are ill prepared for our role as a mourner. Even in the case of several losses over a lifetime, each loss carries with it a distinct response from us because of the unique quality of the relationship that was lost due to death. There is no rehearsal for being a mourner. There is no rehearsal that can prepare us for a difficult loss.

Although the style and length of grieving is definitely culturally based, with religious and social customs giving permission or providing distraction from the actual effects of grief, the process of mourning cannot be directed from outside. If you yourself are not in mourning, but find yourself giving solace to the bereaved, you must be careful and sensitive to move through the mourning process in the framework in which the mourner moves. Time for the expression of feelings as well as a respite from the exhaustive grief work ahead must be balanced with one's ability and readiness to be of help. The empathy which allows one to appreciate the relationship experienced with the deceased must also be part of the healing balance that is necessary for the eventual recovery of the mourner. The ability to grieve with the mourner will prepare the caregiver to ultimately share the mourner's joy, as Kahlil Gibran so eloquently expressed it:

> Then a woman said, speak to us of Joy and
> Sorrow, and he answered: Your joy is your
> sorrow unmasked. And the self-same well
> from which your laughter rises was often
> times filled with your tears.

Mourning Is an Outward Expression

> Tearing his clothes and putting sackcloth around his
> waist, Jacob mourned for his son for many days.
>
> (Gn 37:34)

Throughout recorded history, we read how people have given
outward expression to the grief they felt after the death of a loved
one. In mourning his son Joseph, whom he thought had died in
the desert, Jacob tore his clothes, set aside his daily activities and
allowed himself to grieve. At first glance, some may consider his
response to be somewhat extreme. Others may feel that one or
more of his responses was out of place, e.g., the mourning garb
that he used, or the tearing of his clothes, or the fact that his grief
lasted many days.

While we experience grief in our own unique way, we do
mourn in the cultural patterns that we have known and that have
supported us throughout much of our lifetime. Jacob, in his
mourning, was following the customs of the Jewish people who,
beginning with their forefathers, set aside time to experience
their grief. They embraced mourning not out of fear, but as a
necessary part of the healing process in which ritual and remem-
bering played important roles. The religious aspect of the process was incorporated into the culture. The Jewish people begin
their first response to mourning in the week immediately following a death. For one week in the period called SHIVA, the
survivors gather in the home of the significant other to recall
through memory and storytelling the life and relationship experienced with the deceased. Family members, friends, co-work-
ers, and neighbors pay a Shiva call to offer support and thus
become a part of the healing journey. The storytelling assists one
through the shock and denial that is often associated with the
immediate reactions following a death. There is, in the Orthodox
tradition of Judaism, a 30-day mourning period called the
SHLOSHIM, which continues remembrance of the dead and the
curtailing of certain activities while time and energy is devoted

to acknowledgment and prayer over the loss and for the deceased. The formal mourning period is then over, except for an immediate family member when the mourning period extends to a full year. The KADDISH, a liturgical refrain acknowledging the greatness of God, is repeated by the newly bereaved as a sign of their continued faith in God even after the death of a loved one. This prayer-like mantra, which never mentions death, sanctifies the name of God and prays for the coming of His Kingdom. The instinctive calling out to God in reverence and awe has often been related as having a cathartic effect since it raises and releases sorrow through words. This release has been known to ease the pain and burden since it is shared in a community with a group of supporters providing understanding and support in the midst of sorrow.

> Give sorrow words; the grief that does not speak
> Whispers the o'er frought heart and bids it break.
> Shakespeare (*Macbeth*)
> Act IV, Scene iii, Line 209

In exploring the customs of the Jewish people, we observe certain practices that provide time and space for the mourning process to occur. There is a deliberate attempt to engage many people in the process. There is a framework in which one can work out, over time, the painful effects of grief which are bound to occur after a death. Mourning is a time of acknowledgment. You may want to consider how your cultural and religious beliefs have entered into your mourning process. Have you used the supportive practices which have sustained others in the past or are you reluctant to do so because you may think that these mourning rituals may be too painful to bear? Perhaps you may even be using some already established practices which have been borrowed from other customs and religious practices.

There is no one right or wrong way to engage yourself in the mourning process. There is only your way. And the route along the healing journey must be right for you. It must make sense, it must provide understanding, it must help to express what you feel and provide time for adjustment to the new role that you must play after the period of mourning is over. The key is that it was *your* loved one. Only you know the reality of the relationship that must be mourned. The pain that must be expunged because of the anxiety you feel on account of the separation will be released in ways that are "right" for you. The key is that mourning cannot be rushed. You do not have to please others in the process or be able to make it right for others. Even several people in the same household will mourn the same person in different and varied ways. That, too, is normal because each had a different relationship with the deceased. The journey from grief to healing is a deliberate attempt to restore balance and harmony to your life which has changed after the death of your loved one. The journey is your journey walked in companionship with a God who is able to restore peace to your heart in spite of your loss.

Consider Psalm 62 which encourages us to rest in God who is both gentle and strong and who has compassion on those who call upon him in their need:

> In God alone be at rest my soul;
> from him comes my salvation.
> God alone is my rock and my salvation,
> my stronghold: I stand firm.
> In God is my safety and my glory,
> He is the rock of my strength.
> My refuge is in God.
> Trust in God at all times, O my people!
> Pour out your hearts before him;
> for God is our refuge.

The First Phase of Grief
(Shock, Numbness, Disbelief)

When loss comes entirely without warning, an element of shock is experienced. *Shock* is defined as a response to sudden, violent or upsetting emotional and physical disturbance. It is an automatic inner alarm system that warns us that the event to be handled is severe and often emotionally traumatic. Shock is a first-line defense that shields the consciousness from some extremely unpleasant reality, allowing us to gradually come face to face with the full impact. A slowing down of all bodily systems is a common manifestation of shock. Fainting, for example, is not uncommon. Even though one may seem to be dealing with reality by tending to the details regarding funeral arrangements, church services, getting in touch with those who must be informed of the death, and taking care of ordinary tasks such as getting an occasional bite to eat, many people have the sense of being on automatic pilot. So often in the months following death when shock has diminished, mourners recall feeling as though they were mere spectators in the drama unfolding in someone else's life, as if they were playing out a necessary but somehow impersonal role, not really feeling the impact of the reality of their loss. A woman in bereavement counseling after the death of her daughter stated, "This shock must have been a gift from God. It would have been impossible to face the reality of my daughter's death without some kind of emotional anesthesia." Shock is nature's way of protecting the body and mind from the impending blow of reality which may be too difficult to bear at the time. Shock is often followed by two other common grief reactions also designed to moderate the pain of loss, numbness and disbelief.

Numbness and Disbelief

Depending upon one's readiness for the death of a loved one, shock gradually diminishes over time. Slowly, both intellectually and emotionally, the reality of the loss is increased. Mourners begin to go about their daily tasks of life and living, and this normal everyday interaction further impresses upon them that death has actually occurred and that it has happened to their loved one and changed their life forever. This again may be too much to handle at one time. And so we are often given another psychological gift called numbness and disbelief. We don't feel the effects of the loss with the full intensity that will come into play later in the mourning journey. This phase of grief has often been related by bereaved persons as a dreamlike state that allows for the intermingling of thoughts about the loss with other distracting and less painful thoughts and experiences. Concentration at this stage is difficult and some find the dreamlike quality troublesome. A sense of knowing versus not knowing prevents mourners from coming face to face with the full impact of the loss even though there is an acceptance of the reality that the loss has occurred.

Many bereaved persons report a sense of urgency to confront the daily tasks that must be dealt with. They find that these bouts of numbness and disbelief, while helpful in easing the pain of facing reality, actually distract them from moving on with necessary tasks. Here, great patience with oneself must be exercised. If you are confronted with immediate tasks, some imposed by others and some imposed by yourself, give yourself permission to rest now and then along your journey to recovery. If it feels like a desert experience, remember the mind is searching for an occasional oasis for a reason. Permission to pause, to take things one step, one day, at a time, is important. It is here that supportive companionship can play a consequential role by allowing you to engage in reality testing and moving you on to the next phase of the journey through grief.

Spiritually speaking, some bereaved persons report being stuck in a time of faith crisis. "Why?" "Why me?" "How?" "What has happened?" Dismissing these questions seems to compound one's anxiety as numbness and disbelief diminish. The holding pattern created by the desert experience can be real and helpful at this time. Prayer for understanding can be useful on the emotional and psychological levels as you begin your first confrontation with loss. Your questions — all of your questions — are valid and important. While you may find few immediate answers to them, they will help you to discover the true feelings that lie within. Confiding in a trusted listener will help you to explore your questions and diminish the effects of numbness and disbelief, bringing you to a time of acknowledgment and eventual peace.

The Second Phase of Grief
(Alarm and Anxiety)

One reaction to shock is *alarm*. Gradually, as the reality of the loss is increased and as numbness and disbelief begin to subside, alarm and even a sense of panic can make themselves felt. "It is true. The one I so loved is gone for good." The stark realization that death has actually occured and that life has changed forever takes place in many and varied ways.

A client in bereavement counseling called me immediately after a shopping trip to the local supermarket. Claire's husband Dan had died some two months earlier. She had seemed to manage very well as she went through the process of sharing, receiving support, praying, and reading to understand the loss of her husband of 30 years. In the counseling sessions she often said that she was afraid that she was doing too well, yet she was grateful for her strength in the midst of her sadness. However, as she walked to the checkout register with her cart full of groceries, she noticed several items in the cart that were Dan's favorites. Unexpectedly, a tremendous sense of loss came over her. She remembered thinking that she wouldn't need these items anymore. In the flash of a few seconds she remembered how the items were cooked, and how conversations and teasing went on in the kitchen, how sometimes a leisurely meal would last for an hour even though they may have talked over the same events many times before. It was the first time that she silently uttered the words to herself, "My husband is dead."

Claire had gone to the supermarket for a pleasurable experience and a simple desire to shop for food, and encountered something quite unexpected. That simple event, even though two months after the death, caused her alarm and not a little anxiety. She related that her heart raced, she was flushed and warm in her neck and face, and found herself immobile for just a moment. She left the shopping cart in the center aisle and quickly walked four blocks to her home. She reported in a later session that she had left her car in the parking lot and called her daughter at work to pick it up for her on her way home that evening. Claire said that she had only enough strength to crawl into bed hoping to shut out the world. Dan was indeed dead, and now she had to face that fact. But why only now? Simply stated, her initial shock, numbness and disbelief had worn off, giving way to the startling alarm of reality.

Alarm sets off autonomic physical reactions as the mind begins to confront the stark reality of the situation. It was only when Claire became fully aroused by the reality due to a simple everyday reminder of groceries that she was forced, but also enabled, to confront the true reality of the effect of Dan's death. Shock, numbness and disbelief had been protecting Claire from the impact of reality. And though she had been able to function and seemed to be coping quite well in the early days of her mourning, now she had to enter the phase of confrontation with her loss. This confrontation alarmed her and seemed to her like a major setback since she had apparently been doing so well up to now. The early coping was normal and necessary, but only temporary. The reality and truth about the grief journey is that we experience many setbacks along the way towards healing. These are common and can be expected. It is encouraging, though, to know that each setback is not as far back as the preceding one, and all are integral to the healing process. They must occur in order to provide catharsis and eventual relief. Alarm, however, in this phase can cause a generalized anxiety reaction. Hyperactivity and stress can be at an all-time high and the discomfort of anxiety due to alarm can set off a train of reactions leading to fear, uneasiness, and feelings of utter helplessness. Occasionally, a syndrome called "reactive depression" triggers uncontrollable bouts of anxiety and this should prompt contact with a physician.

Understanding alarm as a time-limited reaction may be helpful. Self-relaxation techniques, comfort controls, rest and a moderation of activity can also have a calming effect on grief anxiety. Anxiety is common even for persons who have not experienced anxiety in the past. Consult your own patterns of diet, rest and balance to counter-affect the reality of anxiety. Be assured that relief will come.

The Third Phase of Grief
(Confrontation)

A Time of Confrontation

Personal confrontation with loss often expresses itself as a protest in which we cry out, "No!" to the reality of the loss. In fact, that cry, whether verbal or uttered in silence, is so powerful that it erupts physically, as well as emotionally, and resounds throughout our being. As an infant we learned to protest the absence of our parents through our cries. As a child, we may have protested the taking of things from us by our temper tantrums. As a teenager, we may have given in to mood swings and acting-out behavior. But as we grow into adulthood, the everyday protest against loss requires what many would consider a more appropriate or mature response. In some cases, the absence of articulation may be preferred over direct expression. And yet, we continue to cry out whenever loss is encountered. The intensity, the frequency, and the duration of that cry will be determined by the value, the interest, and the love that is associated with the relationship we had with our loved one.

While adulthood produces a more controlled protest and a less visible response to the normal losses of life, when faced by the trauma of another's death, we can find ourselves at odds with our usual and predictable patterns of response that may have been helpful or supportive in the past. The grief experienced because of the death of a loved one is unlike any other loss. Because of its irreversibility, a predictable search for some

9

culprit (God, the doctor, this type of disease, the person or thing
responsible for the accident) takes place. We are overwhelmed
by a sense of helplessness in the face of death and fear facing the
future. The intensity of grief can be frightening. It represents a
departure from our usual normal sense of well-being.

George Engel, a psychiatrist from the University of Roch-
ester, raised this interesting question in a thought-provoking
essay published in *Psychosomatic Medicine*. Engel's theory is that
the loss of a loved one is psychologically traumatic to the same
extent as being severely burned is physiologically traumatic.
He proposes that just as healing is necessary to bring the body
back into homeostatic balance, a similar period of time is
likewise needed to return a mourner to a similar state of
equilibrium. And as with physical healing, full function or
nearly full function can be restored, but there are also incidents
of impaired healing. Just as the terms healthy and pathological
apply to various courses in physiological healing, Engel argues
that the same terminology may be applied to mourning. He sees
mourning as a process that takes time until grief is diminished
and the full restoration of function can take place. Mourning
carves out a predictable space in one's life called the time of
bereavement. Bereavement, while it represents a departure from
our normal way of living, is a limited period which is to be
considered normal, appropriate and even necessary. Webster's
defines bereavement as ". . . a state of being acutely deprived."
Other dictionaries use the expressions "being robbed,"
"thwarted" and "cheated" out of a predictable situation, cir-
cumstance or period.

The term normal sometimes refers to the expression of
grief during one's time of bereavement. And it is in the maxi-
mum expression of grief at this time that we see the value of
catharsis. As a pastoral psychologist, I am aware of the pain
associated with the expression of grief. In many instances, grief
is put on hold by mourners because they associate the pain as
too destructive to any semblance of well-being. And yet, in the
grief process, mourners are simply responding normally to an

abnormal event — the trauma of being forever separated here on earth from one whom they have loved. As it is normal to know that death will one day separate us, it is also normal to not like the fact that this will one day have to happen. In fact, it is normal to confront and protest this unwelcomed fact of life. Even those with strong faith can legitimately protest this loss. Consider the response of David in Psalm 102.

Psalm 102

O LORD, hear my prayer, and let my cry come to you. Hide not your face from me in the day of my distress. Incline your ear to me; in the day when I call, answer me speedily. For my days vanish like smoke, and my bones burn like fire. Withered and dried up like grass is my heart; I forget to eat my bread. Because of my insistent sighing I am reduced to skin and bone. I am like a desert owl; I have become like an owl among the ruins. I am sleepless, and I moan; I am like a sparrow alone on the housetop.

All the day my enemies revile me; in their rage against me they make a curse of me. For I eat ashes like bread and mingle my drink with tears. Because of your fury and your wrath; for you lifted me up only to cast me down. My days are like a lengthening shadow, and I wither like grass. But you, O LORD, abide forever, and your name through all generations. You will arise and have mercy on Zion for it is time to pity her, for the appointed time has come.

David's experience of loss infers that he was experiencing the anxiety of separation at an intense level — physical, emotional, and spiritual. The upheaval, distress and isolation which he felt represents a departure from a normal state of well-being. Let us consider the three common areas of disturbance in grief: Physical - Emotional - Spiritual. The Psalmist talks about the legitimacy of the pain. And it is in his expression of pain that catharsis takes place. This story is real, powerful and whole-some. From the honest expression of his feelings will come his later expression of understanding and acceptance.

Physical Distress

The Psalmist talked of *physical distress*. Physical (somatic) dis-tress is a common and often the first grief disturbance as the shock, numbness and disbelief begin to subside. It is as if the body were beginning to incorporate the emotional trauma that is being felt by the mind. The distress can be expressed in any of the body systems: cardiovascular, sensory, kinesthetic, mus-cular, gastrointestinal, respiratory, or reproductive. Some com-mon disturbances of grief in the bereavement time include:

. . . Hollowness in the stomach	. . . Tightness in the chest
. . . Throat irritation	. . . Bladder disturbance
. . . Bowel disturbance	. . . Stomach pains
. . . Breathlessness	. . . Body aches
. . . Rashes	. . . Allergy exaggeration
. . . Weakness	. . . Muscle pain
. . . G.I. Tract disturbances	

While psychosomatic or unfounded illness is a possibility, certainly one should consult with a physician if symptoms present a major deviation from one's normal state of well-being. Even though a physical disruption can occur at any time for very short episodes or be expressed as an exacerbation of a chronic condition, persons encountering such reactions during normal phases of bereavement should talk about them when they occur. As we all know, the power of the mind has a strong influence over the physical manifestations of an emotion affect-ing any one of the major body organs. The time of bereavement is difficult enough without letting some or many of these physical realities compound your normal grief anxiety.

Andrew was devastated by the sudden death of his son Alex after an automobile accident. He immediately began experiencing a great deal of chest pain which, even after several contacts with his physician, could not be traced to any specific physical ailment. The body's autonomic nervous system was reacting to the stress of his son's death in a way which is not all that unusual. Knowing that he was not having a heart attack relieved his anxiety somewhat, but what was almost as important in alleviating his symptoms was the time and concern that his doctor showed him in the course of the examination. Andrew recalls feeling better during the exam time in the physician's office when his doctor spoke with him about Alex and the details of the death. From that time on, Andrew's chest pains grew less frequent, but he still had to deal with the pain of his grief and the difficulty of adjusting to life without Alex. His doctor suggested that he seek bereavement counseling in addition to his regularly scheduled physical exams, and this proved to be enormously beneficial.

Another common physical disturbance in grief has to do with sleep. There may be an inability to sleep, a difficulty in falling asleep, or more frequently, an inability to stay asleep. One wakes in the early hours of the morning and remains awake for the rest of the night. This is normal, especially in the early months after the loss, notably after shock, numbness and disbelief have subsided. One way of understanding sleep is to see it as an action that prompts us to let go of control. Bereavement is an event in our life which has ended our control over the life-giving and life-sustaining components of a relationship that were shared with a loved one. The need to remain in control is a defense mechanism against the fear of future loss, as well as replaying out the former lack of control that we exercised at the time of the death of the loved one. Sleeplessness can also be caused by the fear of being overwhelmed with unconscious thoughts and feelings. This can be expressed as fear of possible nightmares, fear of loneliness, as well as fear of what grief reactions may be brought into the next day. Lack of sleep is a

common grief disturbance. Fighting for sleep will often in
crease the original agitation that one feels. A common sugges-
tion has been to get up and move about. The quick or deliberate
change of atmosphere or room has the potential for allowing
the mind to break free from the state of anxiety that may be
induced by the bed or bedroom.

Recently, a patient told me that she slept on the couch for
the first several weeks after the death. Her family insisted that
she return to her bedroom where proper rest could take place.
Sheryl decided not to listen to the many suggestions that she
received from well-intentioned relatives and friends, but to
proceed with her pattern of sleeping on the couch in the living
room. In counseling she discussed the issues and realized that
she felt safer in the living room because it was near the telephone. After all, this was the first time in 20 years that she was
alone in the house. The discomfort of the couch was preferable
to the isolation and fear of not having a telephone within arm's
reach. While it may appear that an extension telephone in the
bedroom would be the solution (and eventually it was), Sheryl
needed to assign meanings to her actions. These motives came
to light over a short period of time with consultation and the
sharing of her feelings and thoughts in therapy. She did eventually return to her bedroom where more comfortable sleep
was possible. In fact, her increased sleep decreased her irritabil-
ity with others and provided for a better entry to the next day
of work and interaction with others. She felt physically rested
and well, and noticed that her increased physical energy altered
many of her physical patterns of grief as well. She needed time
to clarify and to understand her feelings and subsequent reactions.

Weight loss can be a normal grief reaction following the
death of a loved one providing that it is not too great and does
not continue too long. It is too great if it results in increased
weakness and too long if it complicates the necessary routines
of life and living. Ed relates that when his young daughter died
he recalls feeling, "This loss is too hard to swallow." And this

feeling actually interfered with his ability to swallow during the process of eating. Other physical complaints include a lack of appetite, no taste in the eating of food, and digestive inconsistencies from frequent bowel movements to chronic constipation. Again, consultation with a physician may be in order, but knowledge about the effects of grief on the body should prevent unnecessary fears or the exaggeration of symptoms.

Respiratory distress arouses further anxiety and may also lead one to seek medical attention. Breathlessness or the feeling of not being able to breathe regularly or deeply enough complicates a need for usual daily interaction. These episodes may appear frequently for a few seconds or regularly, especially when fear is induced as the topic of the death or feelings about your deceased loved one surface. The anxiety brought on by breathlessness can often be alleviated simply by talking about your feelings with another. The emotional release that comes about through such sharing decreases physical distress and alleviates much psychic pain and physical disturbance.

Crying and the Effects of Its Release

Contrary to popular belief, tears of grief are not a sign of a chronic "feeling sorry for oneself" but are rather episodes of acute anxiety brought on by the yearning for a loved one who is deceased. The expression "a pang of grief" describes the pain associated with such a loss. Sobbing expresses very dramatically the acute pain experienced by the mourner. It is a negated form of weeping; although the cry itself is muted, the spasmodic respiratory movement remains. This is often seen in the young child before and after weeping occurs. It is similar to the deep sighing often experienced by those who mourn. The psychic pain becomes "too much to handle" and is released through tears and sobs and sighs. Even the facial grimace in grief reflects a compromise between the urge to cry and the urge to suppress such unadult-like behavior. Should these things

occur, relax and feel the great release which comes up from
down deep. Release of pent-up emotions in these ways is
generally very healthy. Don't be afraid to express your grief this
way.

The inhibition of fears is often a learned behavior having
been imposed upon us from our early development. Consider
the expressions:

> Be brave. . . don't cry.
> Be a little soldier for me now. . . don't cry.
> Big boys don't cry.
> Don't let your loved one see you weeping
> . . . it would upset them in heaven.

As I recall some of these expressions, I am assuming that I have
heard them in my own lifetime from well-intentioned others
who desired to spare me of certain pain, or perhaps to spare
themselves from their own helplessness in the presence of one
who is crying. Tears have a tendency to frighten others away.
And yet, would we try to prohibit the expression of pain in
other physical disturbances? Many view tears as something
that can be regulated by the mourner. Often they cannot be
controlled. The ability to tolerate pain without tears is often a
learned behavior in childhood. Tears should not be measured
or discounted. They, too, are a normal part of grief's response
to loss. Bereavement is a time of great vulnerability, and tears
are an expression of our vulnerability. I often ask individuals
and group members in counseling to allow their tears to speak
to them. If their tears could be put into words, what would they
be saying now? Your response may help you to understand
your own pain, fear, confusion and vulnerability better. Understanding the physical reactions associated with the pain of grief
may be the first big step along the healing journey. In fact, pain
is a necessary and valid part of the journey to recovery. It will
occur whether we discount it, desire it or ignore it. The course
of action is to go through it, with support, respite, release and
understanding.

The Fourth Phase of Grief
(Emotional Upheaval)

Searching, Denial and Distortion

One of the most confusing phases of the normal response to grief is the bereavement experience of *searching*. Even the term itself does not give a clue to what is truly being thought and felt by the mourner. You might ask, "Searching for what? Or whom?" Is denial so strong that people actually believe their loved one is not dead? In the worst case scenario some of that could be true. *Denial* is a defense mechanism at work to ease the pain by unconsciously blocking out the reality of the death. In other cases, denial could be described as a desire to know and not know the reality of the loss. It is the mind's way of initially dealing with some of the more painful aspects of the truth. Denial allows truth to be filtered into the consciousness one layer at a time. As the mourner begins to process information about the death, a respite is sometimes needed so that the person can assimilate some of the starker aspects of the reality confronting him or her. In cases where death has been sudden and traumatic, denial is often a healthy mechanism to get from the moment of acknowledgment to the next phase of admission. Denial is not a full-blown delusion and should be recognized for what it is, a simple defense mechanism, usually temporary in duration, which enables one to gradually cope with the reality of death or dying.

We are told in the bereavement accounts of Queen Victoria

that she had Prince Albert's shaving gear laid out for him each morning in the year after his death, and went about the palace speaking to him. She was in a classic state of denial.

Distortion is another defense mechanism which, for a time, buffers the full blow of reality when the mourner is not quite ready for such an enormous confrontation. Reality is temporarily distorted. Unconscious impulses are given conscious expression. Dreams seem real. Again, slight distortion is not delusion. Since most of my daily tasks are in bereavement and hospice settings, I have a healthy respect for the many levels of denial that are expressed in the bereavement process and a great deal of patience and empathy for time-limited reactions and responses to stress. I find it helpful to encourage my patients to give free rein to their reactions to an impending or actual loss. It is in the living out of a response that we are later able to revisit the wounded area of life and to question its place and importance in the broader scope of things. As long as the responses are not life-threatening, physically or psychologically, I would rather assume the role of a companion on the grief journey rather than that of an obstacle along the way.

Disorganization

- A feeling of going through the emotions of living — not living
- Inability to initiate any activity — exhaustion
- Confusion and feelings of unreality — disbelief
- A fear of mental illness — exaggerated fear
- Effort to accomplish previously routine tasks — helplessness
- Lack of interest in daily activities
- Preoccupation with the thoughts and images of the deceased
- A feeling that time is suspended
- A compulsion to speak of the loss
- A compulsion to find out details regarding the loss

Mourning is a gradual process whereby the events of the loss become real and are acknowledged as such by the mourner only through time. There is much frustration as the truth is sought, denied and distorted. While mourning is necessary to the full process of recovery after loss, it is also exhaustive work. The internal and external world which once made sense has been forever changed and modified. This, too, leads to frustration. But the frustration gradually gives way to acceptance, recovery and healing. Eventually, denial, distortion and disorganization are replaced by a keen awareness of reality, thus ending the search that appeared so necessary when the mourning journey began.

A poem by Edna St. Vincent Millay sensitively describes how painful the process is when one passes from denial to acknowledgment, and hence how necessary the support of caregivers who understand:

> Time does not bring relief; you all have lied
> who told me time would ease me on my pain!
> I miss him in the weeping of the rain;
> I want him at the shrinking of the tide;
> The old snows melt from every mountain-side,
> and last year's leaves are smoke in every lane;
> But last year's bitter loving must remain
> heaped on my heart, and my old thoughts abide.
> There are a hundred places where I fear to go,
> so with his memory they brim.
> And entering with relief some quiet place
> where never fell his foot or shone his face
> I say, There is no memory of him here!
> And so stand stricken, so remembering him.

Preoccupation with the Events of Loss

Bereavement has also been viewed as a time of rumination over the loss. Preoccupation with the loss seems to always be in the forefront of the mind and repeated *reality testing* is the only way through this often difficult phase of the mourning process. Reality testing is best described as a repetitious review of the events surrounding the loss and the role of the deceased and yourself in the midst of the loss. Some would consider this too painful a process to bear, but reality testing with a trusted friend or helper can eventually clear up misconceptions or untruths. The obsessional review is indeed painful, but it cannot be wished away or suppressed if eventual healing and recovery are sought. You may go repeatedly over each step that led to the loss. "Did we make the right choice of a physician or of a hospital?" "Did the 911 Emergency Team arrive in an expected time frame?" "Why did I wait to call for help?" "What was he or she thinking of me?" And on and on. Unpleasant memories may continue to rise to the surface. It has been my experience as a helper to many bereaved persons that you will need to find a trusted friend — even just one who will really be of help — who will give you the permission you need to review your loss. Putting words to your feelings and questions helps legitimize the loss. It is in the owning of the loss that the process of grieving moves towards accommodation and acceptance.

Normal Thought Patterns In Grief

Preoccupation	Rumination	Lack of Self-Esteem
Dreams	Isolation	Loneliness
Denial	Disbelief	Numbness

The Fifth Phase of Grief
(Encountering the Feelings of Grief)

Most people think that grief is primarily sorrow, and that sorrow is experienced only in sadness and depression. Throughout the last several decades, helpers of the bereaved in both clinical and pastoral settings have shared numerous findings relating to the fact that strong feelings and emotional upheavals are not only common, but necessary in the full scope of the healing process. Some major grief reactions common to the mourning process are:

. . . Anger	. . . Fear
. . . Helplessness	. . . Yearning
. . . Relief	. . . Guilt
. . . Rage	. . . Shame

Anger

Anger is common and normal in almost all life experiences. When someone you love dies, it is very common to feel angry. Many people will not admit to feelings of anger if you inquire directly about it. Identifying the strong feelings of grief such as anger will help you to understand your mourning journey as it begins to unfold. Holding onto a strong feeling such as anger without identifying its source will not present a full picture of the true feelings surfacing in the bereavement experience. Anger is a result of being threatened or having that which you love and value threatened. Death is a final act of separation. The threat is imminent, as well as future-oriented. Because of the unusual pressures associated with dying and death, we are angry at the mere fact that death has interrupted a relationship. Whether death was welcomed in the sense of suffering being alleviated or vehemently protested in the event of an unexpected death, the results of anger can still be the same. It is important to share your tale of loss since the meaning of the relationship, as well as the meaning that the death holds for you, will emerge through your story.

The direction of anger is a key factor in the expression of grief. Anyone who contributed to the separation causing death could emerge as a target in grief: God, the doctors, the hospital, the emergency squad, and so forth. There have been occasions when anger is directed at the deceased — for leaving, getting ill, not taking care of him/herself, for not warning you, loving you and ultimately for abandoning you. The pronouns of grief, if you listen carefully are: I — Me — and My, indicating the personalized assault that is confronted in the face of death. When undefined issues of dependency present themselves, mourners have an extremely difficult time with anger. Ambivalent relationships will also bring heightened anger into play in the face of death.

At a recent group counseling session in our parish center, there was a noticeable silence by Florence, a rather active and vocal group member. The subject shifted to anger and most group members rejected the idea that they would be angry at their deceased spouses under any circumstances whatsoever. It was only Rita who came close to what she described as casual annoyance due to Ralph's intermittent snoring. Florence shifted her position on the sofa several times and nodded politely in response to the others. Noting her uncomfortableness with the subject, I decided to invite her to remain after the session to give her some time for personal exploration. She readily agreed, and after shedding a few light tears — all the while searching for my approval, she related that her husband was a manic-depressive and that it took a toll on her life throughout the course of his illness. She continued speaking of her feelings of isolation throughout her 30-year marriage and the effects of daily verbal and emotional abuse and uncertainty. Florence had suffered much in her relationship with Ed. She was angry with Ed for having made her life such a hell for so long and relieved that his death brought an end to her years of suffering. These were two feelings that she felt could not be shared with the others because they probably would not be understood by this nice group of ladies who always had such nice things to say about their husbands. She thought that it would be unloving and unfaithful to Ed if she disclosed the reality of their relationship since it was a well-kept secret in the community.

Florence continued private counseling for a few brief sessions in which she came to terms with her relationship with Ed and her loss. She learned that her anger was not only appropriate but normal under such circumstances. Several weeks later, Florence asked for some time in the group to share a thought. All ears perked up as she began by saying that she may have missed out several weeks earlier by not participating in the discussion on anger. Florence continued and told her story. There were some tears of empathy from the group for her and also for Ed who had suffered with such a misunderstood illness. Later on in the session, Emily added that there were a few angry moments in her time of caregiving while George was in the hospital. The group later accepted anger as valid and legitimate.

Anger is a normal and natural reaction by nice people who have to face difficult circumstances. Anger doesn't have to end with more anger, however. It can be released in a wholesome way, be understood and integrated into our lives. The Bible speaks of the righteous anger of God which enabled the world to change. However, it also tells us that following God's anger came mercy, and following the anger expressed by Jesus came forgiveness.

Guilt

Guilt and self-reproach are common experiences of bereaved persons. Guilt can also be one of the greatest obstacles in overcoming grief. It can arise from a number of beliefs and can be conscious or unconscious, recognized or well-hidden due to self-reproach and shame. Guilt after a terminal illness arises from a futile attempt by a survivor to reassure themselves that everything possible had been done to combat the illness as well as to provide supportive care during the time of dying. Guilt does not need to be realistic or logical. The focus of most guilt arises out of an ongoing desire to protect the loved one at any cost. Subsequent to death, the mind cannot provide enough data to say, "The relationship is over now — you can get on with your life." Guilt is the mind's way of remaining in the relationship with a task to accomplish on behalf of the deceased. The nature of the relationship, though severed through death, is not clear for survivors for sometime after the loss. Remaining in the relationship means to continue to exercise control in the deceased's life. Guilt provides the vehicle for keeping the relationship alive. In fact, it is a distraction from coming face to face with the full impact of the loss.

Carla is a college student who came to us after the suicide of her sister. She described Emma as one who continuously pulled attention-getting stunts to control the household and to get her own way with her parents. When told of her sister's accident (not yet reported as a tragic suicide), she decided to remain in New England rather than to go home to New York and the hospital. She told us that she did not want to give in to another attention-getting stunt — thereby giving in again to Emma. When she learned of the death and especially that it was a suicide, Carla was furious. However, her rage — which was legitimate —was not directed at Emma during the entire first year of grief. It was directed at herself. She felt guilty — guilty for not arriving at the hospital sooner, for not being kinder to Emma, for not acting on Emma's behalf more often. These intense feelings of guilt later evolved into a deep sense of shame. What would others think about a family who did not hear the suicidal cries for help from a daughter and sister? Gently, and with some assistance, Carla was able to reconstruct her own turbulent relationship with Emma. She learned how to express her anger as well as to evaluate her own relationship and interaction with her sister. She questioned her own feelings about caretaking and about her responsibility toward Emma that had been instilled in her since childhood. Guilt can be induced by others, and Carla was reacting to a relationship that was defined by her parents many years prior to Emma's young adult life crisis.

Guilt can arise from a feeling that one should be omnipotent and thus able to have prevented the loss. All of us, in some form or another, feel responsible for a loved one's well-being and safety. "If only" and "what if" questions arise in most situations after a death. Our desire to protect and save the lives of those we love are normal and natural. If we had information and if we knew of an impending illness or danger, we would all act on behalf of our loved ones. One of the consoling thoughts along our healing journey is that we were responding to the situation with the information that we had. Guilt can be felt in most aspects of normal grief. Guilt can also be exaggerated. We can feel that engaging in the pleasures of life now is unfair, selfish and uncaring. We can accuse ourselves of betrayal, of forgetting the relationship that existed, when we go about doing things that we would normally do. There may also be guilt over feelings of relief associated with a loss. This can happen following the death of a loved one after a long illness, or where caregiving tasks had become intolerably burdensome or unpleasant. If we ever expressed a wish for a loved one's death, we may feel as if the wish caused the event and, therefore, we are guilty. Survivor guilt is another common experience along the journey from grief to healing.

When parents lose a child, we often see extreme examples of survivor guilt. Parents never expect to outlive their child —

no matter the child's age. In the loss of a child, the natural order of life has been subverted. When death happens in an out-of-the-ordinary way, the survivors need more than usual support and encouragement during the healing process. Most parents take some time in going through the necessary reality testing after a child's death; peer and professional counseling can be most helpful in such circumstances.

In reviewing guilt, most of us believe that we could have done more in our relationship with our loved one. Who hasn't felt that way? Perhaps you were doing the appropriate thing at the time you were involved in the circumstances of your loved one's life. Maybe you were as involved as was humanly possible. Perhaps you were where God needed you to be at that particular point in time. What would you advise or say to one in similar circumstances? A perceptive individual once said, "I believe that God forgives you; now the hard part is to forgive yourself!"

Loneliness

In his study of relationships, Robert Weiss of Harvard University points out two kinds of loneliness: the loneliness of emotional isolation and the loneliness of social isolation. The loneliness of emotional isolation is experienced when we lose a person who has provided us with a sense of security and belonging. It brings us back to the initial sense of attachment that bonded us to our parents and family from infancy. The loneliness of social isolation is experienced when the loss ends our ability to respond to others and to be involved with them in meaningful interaction. These two kinds of loneliness can happen singularly or simultaneously.

There are times when loneliness brings on low self-esteem because the lost relationship was the key that provided stimulation for self-assessment and the important feedback that we all need. Frank is a neighbor whose backyard adjoins my yard.

He used to relish the fall and leaf-raking which he said prepared him for his favorite feast of the year — Thanksgiving. Following the death of his wife Doris, Frank paid little attention to his grounds-keeping activities. Speaking over the fence one weekend afternoon, I questioned him about not seeing him proudly ride on his small tractor — obviously not calling out to Doris, "More iced-tea." Frank said, "Of course, I could do those things that once kept me busy, but who is going to tell me what a wonderful job I have done?"

Feelings of loneliness and isolation are felt to the core of our very being. They are an ongoing reminder of the lost relationship as well as of the need to adjust to a whole new world in the midst of our loss. Grieving takes place on many levels. As Frank learned, it was notably the death of his spouse, but also how that loss affected every part of his being, that made him feel so lonely. Her way of responding to him was unique. Relationships like this take many years to build. They sustain, nourish, and provide that which makes life worth living — loving contact with one who knows me well. We want and we need to feel close to another. Loneliness is the absence of closeness. Intimacy is felt on many levels in relationships. The death of a loved one severs the capacity for intimacy. It takes time and trust to invest in intimacy again. Trust your inner time-clock. Be patient with yourself and with others. Understanding yourself and your needs is the first step towards intimacy.

Loneliness

You left me
unknowing, unthinking
of what I would do without you.
You left me
like a Gypsy leaves a camp.
Since then
minute hands swing around

but the days do not move.
I march on a treadmill
with nowhere to go.
Our circus had closed —
no more high wire acts
Nothing is as it
should be
except this paper
and this paper is sad.

                                        Natasha Lynne Vogdes

Identifying as well as experiencing the loss helps us to claim
ourselves as a sufferer. That in itself is an expression which
describes us at this point in time. Labeling the pain of loneliness
does not exempt us from future suffering, but it puts an indel-
ible mark, now and later on our mourning experience. Owning
the loss experience is being honest with ourselves. We are not
engaging in a "poor me" syndrome (which in itself should not
be discouraged), but we are entering a time of truth telling.
Telling the truth about loneliness makes a bold statement about
what we really believe about ourselves. As a listener, I am quite
encouraged when I hear a client speak of loneliness. It says to
me, "You are a survivor for life." A survivor is one who knows
that he or she is at her best when involved in a caring and loving
relationship with one or several significant others. The true and
honest admission of loneliness is encouraging because it indi-
cates that they are ready to recognize themselves as persons
meant to interact with other persons, that they prefer relationship to isolation. It also provides insight into the avenues of
future healing as they choose how they will engage themselves
with others in the future.

Helplessness

Helplessness is being without power to help yourself. It is the
feeling of being acutely vulnerable, incompetent and weak.

Grief induces a feeling of helplessness from the time of antici-patory grief (before death occurs) to post-loss grief (after death). In a recent bereavement support group, I asked the group members about feelings of helplessness since it was an issue the group had not resolved in previous discussions. Tom looked pleased and said, "Thank God! I thought we would never get back to this topic." He talked about feeling quite independent as a single man in his forties, but the death of his father — his final parent — brought about feelings of weakness, self-doubt, and fear of the future. Tom couldn't understand these recent feelings since he had never experienced weakness or self-doubt before.

Helplessness occurs when loss happens independently of our willing it. It can be extremely frustrating. There are usually two aspects to the feeling — helplessness in longing for what is irretrievable, and helplessness in facing the future without that which was lost. To depend on others is at the core of our human survival. Feeling victimized is one dimension of helplessness. Survivors of a loss often feel themselves to be victims — victims of the death of another. Life, as it was, stopped and future plans for the partnership came to an end. The sense of helplessness is usually temporary. Even the strong have the very core of their strength taken away at the death of a loved one. Tom, for example, called himself an orphan in a later group session. The orphaned adult confronts a past that can never exist again except through memory. For some, this is simply not accept-able. Past issues of abandonment, resolved as well as unre-solved, surface in the presence of current loss and have a definite impact on it. All of these factors should encourage us to mobilize our resources for future survival. It is important to evaluate our coping skills whenever we are challenged by the feeling of helplessness and to properly assess our strengths as we remain open to future changes that will eventually enable growth.

REACTIONS IN THE NORMAL GRIEF EXPERIENCE

• changes in emotions and thought processes
• behavioral changes
• interpersonal and social changes
• physical complaints

I. Physical Sensations

hollowness in stomach
tightness in the chest
tightness in the throat
oversensitivity to noise
sense of depersonalization
breathlessness
weakness in muscles
lack of energy
dry mouth

II. Behaviors

sleep disturbances
appetite disturbances
absent-minded behavior
social withdrawal
dreams of deceased
avoiding reminders of deceased
searching and calling out
sighing
restless overactivity
crying
visiting places/carrying objects of value to the deceased
treasuring objects of the deceased

III. Feelings

anxiety/fear
loneliness
fatigue
shock
yearning
emancipation
relief
numbeness
helplessness

IV. Cognitions

disbelief
confusion
preoccupation
sense of presence
hallucinations

The Sixth Phase of Grief
(Recovery)

Time alone will not heal the wounds of grief. The mourning journey must be dealt with. It is an encounter with rough roads and turns and the course will have detours, straight paths and speed bumps along the way. Grief is the pain of loss becoming real. The secret of being lifted up through grief is to be fully engaged in the mourning process. Understanding your loss requires an ongoing review of what happened to you along the way. Consider these major moments along the path from grief to healing.

Understanding Your Loss

Provide yourself with a review of the illness, the caregiving, the details surrounding the death, and finally the news of the death as you experienced it. After careful review there may not be sufficient or appropriate answers to your questions. This may mean that you will have to learn to live with questions that will have no answers. Understanding your loss enables you to review the past relationship with your loved one. You can review all of the facets of the relationship — positive and negative. That review may be troublesome for some. Understanding your loss means acknowledging it. Acknowledgment leads to acceptance of the loss as well as the depth of the past relationship. Recalling the relationship with your loved one

will help you legitimize the depth of your grief response and
your understanding of that response.

Experiencing the Pain of Your Grief

The various segments of this book have intended to tell the
truth about the many responses along the mourning journey we
call grief. Knowledge can diminish some of the fear you may
have about the nature of your own grief reaction. We each
grieve in our own unique way. Your response — whatever it is
— is normal, valid, and appropriate. Your grief response is part
of the total picture that gives insight into who you are as a
mourner, and it provides you with an understanding of the
significance of your relationship with your loved one. The pain
of grief, as we have stated, makes itself felt physically, emotionally, and spiritually through the mourning process. You were
able to handle the powerful initial reactions of shock, numbness
and disbelief. After the alarm of reality set in, you began to
confront the many moments of separation pain called grief.
Perhaps you are still experiencing some of the painful effects of
your loss. But, you are here. You have survived many rough
moments and you will survive again.

Pain is only part of the grief picture. It is your desert
experience. It is normal and it is a part of the healing process. Do
not allow yourself to be stranded in the desert. Allow supportive persons to come into your life so that you can share the pain
of your grief. "Joy shared is joy increased — grief shared is grief
diminished." David's response in Psalm 102 manifested the
utter despair of pain. It touched him to the very core of his being.
However, he did not allow himself to be forever stranded in the
desert. He recalled the other moments of his life when God's
mercy and love lifted him up beyond the pain. Perhaps you can
recall the times when it didn't seem possible that you would
survive. But you did survive. You are here to tell your story.
God moved with you and in front of you even though the
waters appeared to be uncharted at the time.

Adjusting to a Changed World

A major adjustment period is to be expected following the loss of anyone dear to you because the world you once knew has now changed. An end has taken place that demands a new beginning. That beginning starts even in the clouded days of confusion and uncertainty following that person's death. And yet, you are not alone. How many times did Jesus reach out to those who implored, "Lord, have pity on me"? His words are as valid for you today as they were to his petitioners 2000 years ago: "Do not be afraid. I am with you." "Ask and you shall receive, seek and you shall find, knock and it shall be opened to you." "Let not your hearts be troubled. Have faith in God and faith in me." "If you would come after me, you must take up your cross each day and follow in my footsteps." Those who called out for pity in the Gospel were met by a Jesus who saw their wounds and responded to their pleas. He understood their cry, and acted on their behalf. It is the same Jesus who will act on your behalf in the difficult moments of adjustment along the way.

Many have little patience with those who take time out to throw a "pity party" for themselves. This is because the word "pity" has several implications, some of them negative. As children we exhibited our wounds until someone came by to see them. Children frequently only begin to cry after being hurt when someone notices their pain. They are looking for pity. Pity, though, is not always self-centered. It has value because it engages the support of another as we confront our pain. Don't be afraid to ask for pity when you need it.

When you are uncertain as to what you can or should do next, hold-on because holding on, in the long run, is often the most positive response you can make at the time. Self-discovery is one of the hidden benefits of the mourning process. The adjustment period allows us to take a close look at ourselves. It is a time for learning about one more layer of our personality and soul that makes each one of us unique. It would be unfor-

tunate to go through this loss, grief and mourning without
learning something more about ourselves. The time of adjustment, though uncertain, is a period in which we gradually
engage ourselves in life and living once again. Taking one step
forward and occasionally one step back are not uncommon
experiences on the journey to healing. Do not be frightened.
God has been there before — with others along the same
journey — and He knows the way.

Recovery is that point in the grief process when you give
yourself final permission to move away from the pain and
uncertainty and begin to look ahead. Yes, it is your life. Yes, it
is okay to move beyond the pain. Yes, it is time for mourning to
cease and healing to begin, one step at a time. Our God is a God
of wonder and surprise, a God who understands and supports
us in our time of grief, a God who smiles on our recoveries along
the way. The following poem invites us to be open to the future
yet to be, as we proceed on our journey to full recovery.

Sea Sculpture

I've whittled
a peninsula
out of myself
with bays
and inlets
to anchor in
during the storms.
I've carved
with care.
I've harbors to
cruise on vacation.
With consideration,
I've chiseled sea-breezes
to cool my coastlines
during heatwaves.
I've fashioned my dunes
so they won't wash away.
The oceans keep me guessing.
The final structure is
still under construction.

A Final Word
Loss as an Agent for Change

The seeds for healing lie dormant even in the midst of the physical, emotional, and spiritual upheaval after loss. It is the winter of our loss. Our identity, once so familiar to us, has changed. We are not the same. We may have changed quickly in the face of sudden death, or over months and years as we waited for death to come during a chronic terminal illness. Some say that fate has dealt us the cards and we must play them. Persons of faith know that nothing happens solely by chance, that God is with us through it all, and that somehow "all things work together for the good of those who love God and are called according to his purpose." He knows how to help us turn even the tragedy of death into an opportunity for our growth and healing. How we come to terms with what we believe brings us to the final step of our ongoing healing journey. What has changed and what remains the same are both part of our new life now. The seed out of which this new life will grow may well be something as simple as the sudden awareness that we have spent a night alone and it was okay, or that we have a full shopping cart that just doesn't seem to make sense anymore. We may begin to think, if I have managed to survive the terror of those first few days and nights maybe I'll be able to survive the rest that's yet to come.

Healing happens when you least expect it. In fact it has been an ongoing process since the day the loss occurred. It heralds the springtime of our loss. It began by ritualizing the

loss through religious services, the visits of friends, and the
opportunity to retell our story repeatedly. A woman mourning
the death of her aged mother said, "When mom died I felt as if
I were limping about like an amputee. People told me how
lucky I was to have had her for so long. If I had the guts, I would
have said, 'Even a few more days, weeks or months would have
been better. I needed her so at this point in my life.'" You will
know that you are coming to terms with your bereavement
when the answers to all the questions you have will seem to
make more sense to you now than they did right after the loss.
And in the long run, it is only to you that the reality of the loss
must make sense.

Slowly, ever so slowly, the ability to concentrate returns,
the ability to laugh and to see the humor in things feels good
again, and God's future plans are anticipated with trust and
hope. It is the summertime of our loss. Saint Paul invites us to
not grieve like those with no hope — but to see grief as a step
towards the rest of the unfolding drama called life. It is a life that
has moved from grief to healing. You have been lifted up to
experience the adventure in faith.

Ideas for the Journey

- Be patient with yourself.
- Go gently. Give yourself time. There is no need to rush.
  Much energy is needed for the healing process.
- Don't overextend yourself. Try not to take on too many
  addi-tional responsibilities. One day at a time.
- Let the grieving process run its course. Depression may
  occur and crying is a normal and natural reaction. It
  provides a necessary physical release.
- Rest and exercise can provide a balanced approach to
  healing.
- Have you thought about keeping a diary? It may be a

good way to learn what your feelings mean and a possible way to understand them.

- Change your routine. You will be pleasantly surprised how interesting situations become when you do things differently.
- Plan events to look forward to. A visit, a trip, a lunch, a movie and time to be with friends can be enjoyable.
- Learn something new. Have you wanted to get that driver's license, go back to school, learn something new? Why not begin and soon?
- Do something for someone else. Giving of your time to another, or to a worthwhile cause can do wonders. Be generous to others and to yourself.
- Take time for yourself. Go to a movie. Visit a friend. Laugh once in a while. Put some balance back into your life. **Work-Rest-Read-Pray-Recreate.**
- Don't have unrealistic expectations for yourself. Be the friend to yourself that you would be to another.
- **Read**. There are many excellent books and articles about grief, mourning, and the bereavement experience.
- **Pray**. Prayer is so important in our lives. When we are hurting, we can open our hearts to the pain and loneliness experienced by Jesus himself. Who can forget the moments Jesus called out in prayer to his heavenly Father? In whatever form you feel comfortable, pray.

Bereaved Person's Prayer

We seem to give our loved ones back to you,
Lord. You gave them to us. But just as you
did not lose them in the giving, neither do we
lose them in the return.

You don't give in the same way that the world
gives. What you give you don't take away.
You have taught us that what is yours is ours
also, if we are yours.

Life is eternal, Lord, and your love is
undying. And death is only a horizon. And
a horizon is nothing but the limits of our sight.

Lift us up strong, Son of God, that we may
see farther. Cleanse our eyes that we may see
more clearly. Draw us closer to yourself, that
we may find ourselves closer to our loved ones
who are with you.

And while you prepare a place for them,
prepare us also for that happy place
where you are and where we hope to be —
forever. Amen.

An Affirmation for Those Who Have Lost

I believe there is no denying it; it hurts to lose.
It hurts to lose a cherished relationship with another,
or a significant part of one's own self.
It can hurt to lose that which has united one with the past,
or that which has beckoned one into the future.
It is painful to feel diminished or abandoned,
to be left behind or left alone.
Yet I believe there is more to losing than just the hurt and the pain.
For there are other experiences that loss can call forth.
I believe that courage often appears,
however quietly it is expressed,

however easily it goes unnoticed by others:
the courage to be strong enough to surrender,
the fortitude to be firm enough to be flexible,
the bravery to go where one has not gone before.
I believe a time of loss can be a time of learning unlike any other,
and that it can teach some of life's most valuable lessons:
In the act of losing, there is something to be found.
In the act of letting go, there is something to be grasped.
In the act of saying "good-bye," there is a "hello" to be heard.
For I believe living with loss is about beginnings
as well as endings.
And grieving is a matter of life more than of death.
And growing is a matter of mind and heart and soul
more than of body.
And loving is a matter of eternity more than of time.
Finally, I believe in the promising paradoxes of loss:
In the midst of darkness, there can come a great Light.
At the bottom of despair, there can appear a great Hope.
And deep within loneliness, there can dwell a great Love.
I believe these things because others have shown the way —
others who have lost and then have grown through their
losing, others who have suffered and then found
new meaning.
So I know I am not alone:
I am accompanied, day after night, night after day.

— James E. Miller

Psalm 5

Give ear to my words, O Lord,
give heed to my groaning.
Attend to the sound of my cry,
my King and God.
To you, O Lord, do I pray.
In the morning you hear my voice;
in the morning I offer you my prayer,
my watching and my waiting.

Through the abundance of your steadfast love
I have access to your house.
I bow down before your holy temple
filled with awe.
Lead me in your justice,
because of those who lie in wait for me.
All those whom you protect shall be glad
and ring out their joy.
You shall shelter them,
for in you do they rejoice.
It is you who bless the just;
you surround him with favor as with a shield.

Psalm 23

The Lord is my shepherd;
there is nothing I shall want.
Fresh and green are the pastures
where he gives me repose.
Near restful waters he leads me,
to revive my drooping spirit.
He guides me along the right path;
he is true to his name.
If I should walk in the valley
of the shadow of death
I will fear no evil.
You are there with your rod and your staff;
with these you give me comfort.
You have prepared a banquet for me
in the sight of my foes.
My head is anointed with oil;
my cup overflows.
Surely goodness and kindness shall follow me
all the days of my life.
In the Lord's own house shall I dwell
forever and ever.

Psalm 65

To you our praise is due in Zion, O God.
To you we pay our vows, you hear our prayer.
To you all flesh will come with its burden of sin.
Too heavy for us, our offenses, but you wipe them
away.
Blessed is he whom you choose and call
to dwell in your courts.
We are filled with the blessings of your house,
of your holy temple.
You uphold the mountains with your strength,
you are girded with power.
You still the roaring of the seas,
the roaring of the tides.

Psalm 121

I lift up my eyes to the mountains;
from where shall come my help?
My help shall come from the Lord
who made heaven and earth.
May He never allow you to stumble!
Let Him sleep not, your guard.
No, He sleeps not nor slumbers, Israel's guard.
The Lord is your guard and your shade;
at your right hand He stands.
The sun shall not smite you by day,
nor the moon in the night.
The Lord will guard you from evil,
He will guard your soul.
The Lord will guard your coming and going
both now and forever.

Bereavement Resources

Abbey Press. Publishers of "Care Notes," an excellent series of brochures on a variety of subjects. Caring Place, Abbey Press, St. Meinrad, IN 47557.

Bereavement Magazine, 8133 Telegraph Drive, Colorado Springs, CO 80920. The magazine in grief caregiving, covering a wide variety of subjects in easy-to-read format.

Center for Loss and Life Transition. Provides a variety of books, videos, audio cassettes, newsletter, brochures and training programs, plus a National Speakers Bureau. 3735 Broken Bow Road, Fort Collins, CO 80526.

College of Chaplains. In addition to a national network of caregivers available for assistance, the College offers the resources of "Care Cassettes" and *The Caregiver Journal*. For information on subscriptions, back issues or cassettes, and how to contact a member chaplain in your area, contact The College of Chaplains, 1701 E. Woodfield, Suite 311, Schaumburg, IL 60173. (708) 240-1014.

Compassion Books, 477 Hannah Branch Road, Burnsville, NC 28714. The grief bookstore. The place to contact for books, cassettes and videos on grief. If they don't have it, they can find it.

Connections. A national resource center directed by Rev. Richard Gilbert. The most extensive compilation of bereavement notes, bibliographies, and materials on the national scene. Dick is an engaging speaker with a multi-faceted background in spiritual and bereavement education issues. For materials and presentations: 1504 N. Campbell Ave., Valparaiso, IN 46383. (219) 464-8183.

Hope for Bereaved, 4500 Onondaga Blvd., Syracuse, NY 13219. Contact them about *Hope for Bereaved*; *Love, Mark*; *Love, Mark II*; also ask for their book on support groups, memberships and newsletter.

Kings College Centre for Education About Death and Bereavement. Directed by Dr. John Morgan, this program offers one of the longest running annual conferences on grief, a resource center for the bereaved and those who care for them, and an extensive catalog of resources, especially audio cassettes. 266 Epworth Avenue, London, Ontario, Canada N6A 2M3.

MADD (Mothers Against Drunk Driving). An excellent resource for parents dealing with accidental deaths, as well as siblings and caregivers. They offer a variety of resources, programs and networking. Contact them at P.O. Box 541688, Dallas, TX 75354-1688. (214) 744-MADD. There may be a local contact person in your area.

National Center for Death Education, 777 Dedham Street, Newton Centre, MA 02159. A resource center for many films and videos.

National Catholic Ministry to the Bereaved. 7835 Harvard Avenue, Cleveland, OH 44105. A pastoral organization devoted to equipping the religious community to be more effective caregivers and responders to the bereaved. Starter kit. Membership services. Newsletter. Annual conference. Library of resources. Well worth your membership, individually, as an organization or as a parish.

Saint Paul Center is the ministry representing the work of Patrick Del Zoppo. The national lectures and training programs in Pastoral Bereavement Counseling, as well as other certifying programs are arranged through Saint Paul Bereavement Center. The programs are offered for Diocesan convocations, Funeral Service Industries, Health Care and Educational Programming. 189 Kemball Avenue, Staten Island, NY 10314. (718) 273-4927.

Thanatos, P.O. Box 6009, Tallahassee, FL 32302. A fine magazine offering helpful resources in grief in a quality format.

The Compassionate Friends. International organization concerned with the grief needs of parents and siblings. Many books, audio and video cassettes and brochures, area chapters, national annual conferences. National Office: P.O. Box 3696, Oak Brook, IL 60522-3696.

The National Childhood Grief Institute. 6200 Colonial Way, Edina, MN 55346. Provides training and education for those who work with children.

Willow Green, A unique resource center offering the best national materials in the area of video works for the bereaved and the general community. Dr. Jim Miller invites the mourner into a community of faith and wholeness with his writings, books and meditative pieces of audio-visual presentation. P.O. Box 25180, Ft. Wayne, IN 46825. (219) 424-7916.

Notes